The Bipolar Disorder Guide 101: Understanding Bipolar Disorder, Types, Symptoms, and Diagnosis

By

Dr. Emily k Pitts

Disclaimer

The information provided in "The Bipolar Disorder Guide 101: Understanding Bipolar Disorder, Types, Symptoms, and Diagnosis" is for educational purposes only and is not a substitute for professional medical advice, diagnosis, or treatment. Always seek the assistance of a trained healthcare expert with any questions you may have regarding a medical problem.

About the author

Dr. Emily K. Pitts, a well-known psychiatrist and author, has recently published a book titled "The Bipolar Disorder Guide 101: Understanding Bipolar Disorder, Types, Symptoms, and Diagnosis." In this book, she goes into the nuances of bipolar disease. As a result of his many years of clinical experience, Dr. Pitts provides patients, caregivers, and professionals working in the field of mental health with a resource that is both insightful and comprehensive. Her guide provides an approachable discussion of diagnostic criteria as well as an overview of the many forms of bipolar disorder and a summary of the most important symptoms. Because of Dr. Pitts's knowledge and compassionate attitude, her book is an indispensable resource for comprehending and coping with bipolar disorder. It offers helpful counsel for managing this hard condition, which would otherwise be difficult to manage.

Table of contents

Introduction
- bipolar disorder: What is it?
- Bipolar Disorder: Historical Views
- The Significance of Comprehending Bipolar Disorder

1. Types of Bipolar Disorder
- Features and Diagnosis of Bipolar I Disorder
- Bipolar II Disorder: Characteristics and Identification
- Cyclothymic Disorder: Symptoms and Assessment
- Other Bipolar and Related Disorders, Both Specified and Unspecified

2. Mania: Signs and Symptoms of Bipolar Disorder Symptoms
- Symptoms and Signs of Hypomania
- Signs and Symptoms of Depression
- Signs and Symptoms of Mixed Episodes

3. **Bipolar Disorder Diagnosis**
- Preliminary Evaluation: Clinical Interviews and Questionnaires
- DSM-5 Guidelines for Diagnostic Criteria
- Differential Diagnosis: Setting Apart from Other Mental Health Conditions
- The Significance of Physical Examination and Medical History

4. **Effect on Daily Life**
- Implications for Personal Relationships
- Difficulties in Work and School Environments
- Organizing Daily Schedules and Self-Care

5. **Care and Handling**
- Pharmacological Therapies: Drugs and Their Applications
- Alternatives to CBT and DBT in psychotherapy
- Adjustments to Lifestyle and Practices for Self-Management
- The Value of Support Systems

Introduction

The complicated mental health condition known as bipolar disorder, which was originally known as manic-depressive illness, is marked by significant mood fluctuations, including emotional highs (mania or hypomania) and lows (depression). An individual's capacity for clear thinking, energy levels, and activity levels, as well as their sleep patterns, are all impacted by this illness. The chronic nature of bipolar disease, along with the potential severity of the condition, makes it an important public health concern. Bipolar disorder affects thousands of persons all over the world.

bipolar disorder: What is it?

Bipolar disorder is a psychiatric illness typified by cycles of manic and depressive episodes. Manic episodes are characterized by times of abnormally heightened mood, increased activity or energy, and other symptoms such as inflated self-esteem, decreased need for sleep, talkativeness, racing thoughts, distractibility, and participating in risky behaviors. Individuals who have manic episodes are more likely to engage in risky behaviors. Episodes of depression, on the other hand, are characterized by periods of poor mood, exhaustion, feelings of worthlessness or guilt, and a loss of interest in the majority of activities. There are several subtypes of bipolar disorder, such as cyclical disorder, bipolar I disorder, and bipolar II disorder. Each of these subtypes is distinguished by the pattern and severity of symptoms that they exhibit.

History of Bipolar Disorder: Perspectives from the Past

Historically, the understanding of bipolar disorder has progressed dramatically. Ancient manuscripts from Greece and Rome depict mood disorders, with physicians like Hippocrates recognizing the occurrence of what we now recognize as bipolar symptoms. However, it wasn't until the 19th century that French doctor Jean-Pierre Falret characterized "circular insanity," a condition with alternating episodes of mania and depression, establishing the framework for modern conceptions of bipolar disorder. In the early 20th century, the term "manic-depressive illness" was coined by Emil Kraepelin, a German psychiatrist, to reflect the cyclical nature of the disorder. This terminology lingered until the latter part of the 20th century, when "bipolar disorder" became the favored word, reflecting a more sophisticated understanding of the condition's spectrum.

The Significance of Comprehending Bipolar Disorder

Understanding bipolar disorder is vital for various reasons. Firstly, it permits precise diagnosis and appropriate treatment, which can considerably enhance the quality of life for people affected. Effective management frequently involves a combination of medication, psychotherapy, lifestyle changes, and support. Secondly, awareness and comprehension of bipolar disease help eliminate stigma and misconceptions surrounding mental health, providing a more supportive atmosphere for individuals to seek care. Lastly, recognizing bipolar disease aids ongoing research efforts aimed at finding the biochemical, genetic, and environmental elements contributing to the disorder, potentially leading to more effective and individualized therapies in the future. Recognizing the multidimensional character of bipolar disorder underlines the significance of a comprehensive and empathic approach to addressing the needs of people living with this condition.

Chapter 1

Types of Bipolar Disorder 1

Bipolar illness is a multidimensional mental health problem that appears in numerous forms, each with specific patterns of mood shifts, symptom intensity, and duration. Understanding these variations is critical for correct diagnosis and effective therapy. The basic kinds of bipolar disorder include Bipolar I Disorder, Bipolar II Disorder, and Cyclothymic Disorder. Additionally, there are other identified and unnamed bipolar and associated diseases that do not fit cleanly into these categories but nonetheless display considerable mood dysregulation.

Features and Diagnosis of Bipolar I Disorder

Bipolar I Disorder is characterized by the occurrence of at least one manic episode, which may be preceded or followed by hypomanic or significant depressive episodes. A manic episode is a distinct time of unusually and persistently elevated, expansive, or irritable mood, lasting at least one week (or any duration if hospitalization is necessary), and is accompanied by at least three (or four, if the mood is simply irritable) of the following symptoms:

1. Inflated self-esteem or grandiosity

2. Decreased need for sleep (e.g., feeling rested after only three hours of sleep)

3. More talkative than usual or feeling pressure to keep chatting

4. Flight of ideas or subjective sense that thoughts are racing

5. Easily distracted

6. Improvement in goal-oriented activity(either socially, at work or school, or sexually) or psychomotor agitation

7. Excessive involvement in activities that have a high potential for painful outcomes (e.g., excessive spending sprees, sexual indiscretions, stupid business ventures)

A diagnosis of Bipolar I Disorder needs the manic episode to produce severe impairment in social or occupational functioning, or to warrant hospitalization to avert damage to oneself or others, or to include psychotic symptoms. These manic episodes are generally followed by depressive episodes, which can be severe and debilitating. During depressed episodes, individuals may suffer chronic sorrow or emptiness, loss of interest in most activities, severe weight changes, insomnia or hypersomnia, exhaustion, feelings of worthlessness or guilt, difficulties concentrating, and frequent thoughts of death or suicide.

Bipolar II Disorder: Characteristics and Identification

Bipolar II Disorder is defined by the presence of at least one hypomanic episode and at least one severe depressive episode. Hypomanic episodes are similar to manic episodes but are less intense and do not produce considerable impairment in social or occupational functioning. To be diagnosed as hypomania, the elevated or irritated mood must remain for at least four consecutive days and be present most of the day, practically every day. The symptoms of hypomania involve the same criteria as mania but to a lower degree:

1.Inflated self-esteem or grandiosity

2.Decreased need for sleep

3.Increased talkativeness

4. Flight of ideas

5. Distractibility

6. Increased goal-directed activity

7. Excessive involvement in risky activities

A crucial distinction is that hypomanic episodes do not result in the substantial functional impairment found in full-blown mania. However, the depressive episodes in Bipolar II disorder tend to be more frequent and severe compared to bipolar I disorder, typically leading to significant functional impairment and higher risks of suicidal ideation and conduct.

Cyclothymic Disorder: Symptoms and Assessment

Cyclothymic Disorder, or Cyclothymia, is characterized by continuous oscillations in mood involving many periods of hypomanic symptoms and times of depression symptoms that are not severe enough to meet the criteria for a major depressive episode. These mood swings must persist for at least two years (one year in children and adolescents) and be present for at least half the time, with the individual not being symptom-free for more than two months at a time.Symptoms of hypomanic phases in Cyclothymia may include:

1. elevated mood;

2. increased self-confidence;

 3. decreased need for sleep;

4. more energy and activity than usual;

5. being more talkative or sociable;

6. engaging in risky behavior.

During depressive stages, symptoms could include:

1. Feeling depressed or hopeless;

2. Fatigue or poor energy;

3. Decreased activity and motivation;

4. Poor concentration;

5. Changes in sleep patterns; the

6. Feelings of worthlessness

While Cyclothymic Disorder is less severe than Bipolar I and II Disorders, it can nonetheless lead to significant suffering and impairment in social, occupational, or other critical areas of functioning if left untreated. The chronic nature of the condition can interfere with personal relationships and professional life, stressing the significance of correct diagnosis and care.

Other Bipolar and Related Disorders, Both Specified and Unspecified

Apart from the basic categories, there are other bipolar and related diseases recognized by mental health professionals. These categories help represent the complete spectrum of mood dysregulation that does not fit neatly into Bipolar I, Bipolar II, or Cyclothymic Disorder.

Other Specified Bipolar and Related Disorders

This category is used when the individual shows symptoms suggestive of bipolar and associated disorders that cause severe distress or impairment but do not match the full criteria for any of the particular illnesses. Examples include:

1. Short-duration hypomanic episodes (2–3 days) with significant depression episodes.

2.Hypomanic episodes with insufficient symptoms and significant depressive episodes.

3.Hypomanic episode without antecedent major depressive episode.

4.Short-duration cyclothymia (less than 24 months).In these circumstances, doctors explain a precise rationale why the presentation does not match the criteria for a more specific diagnosis, ensuring that the distinctive manifestations of mood dysregulation are acknowledged and treated effectively.

Unspecified Bipolar and Related Disorders

This category is used in circumstances where the mood symptoms do not fully fulfill the criteria for any specific bipolar or associated disease and the doctor chooses not to define the reason, typically due to limited information or an emergency context. Examples include:

1. Rapid mood swings without reaching full criteria for hypomania or despair.

2. Atypical presentations of mood disorders.Unspecified bipolar and related disorders allow flexibility in identifying and treating patients with complicated or atypical mood symptoms, ensuring that they receive appropriate care even when their illness does not fit established diagnostic classifications.

- Bipolar disorder comprises a range of mood disorders that vary in severity, duration, and influence on everyday functioning. From the full-blown manic episodes of bipolar I disorder to the less extreme but nevertheless disruptive hypomanic and depressed episodes of bipolar II disorder and the chronic mood changes of cyclical mood disorders, each form requires thorough assessment and appropriate treatment approaches. Additionally, recognizing additional identified and unspecified bipolar and associated diseases ensures that all patients experiencing major mood dysregulation receive proper attention and care. Understanding the intricacies of these diseases is vital for mental health practitioners to provide accurate diagnosis, effective treatments, and compassionate support for people impacted by bipolar disorder.

Chapter 2

Mania: Signs and Symptoms of Bipolar Disorder Symptoms

Mania is a distinguishing aspect of bipolar I disorder and indicates a condition of heightened mood, energy, and activity that can greatly impede an individual's capacity to operate. Understanding the signs and symptoms of mania is vital for the diagnosis and management of bipolar illness.

Symptoms of Mania

Manic episodes are characterized by a discrete time of unusually and consistently high, expansive, or irritated mood and increased goal-directed activity or energy lasting at least one week (or any duration if hospitalization is necessary). The symptoms of mania can be severe and include:

1. Inflated self-esteem or grandiosity: Individuals may demonstrate an exaggerated sense of their abilities, achievements, or importance. They might believe they have exceptional talents or powers.

2.Decreased Need for Sleep: During a manic episode, individuals often feel rested after only a few hours of sleep or may go for days without sleeping and still not feel exhausted.

3. Increased Talkativeness: There is a notable increase in speech, with people talking swiftly, loudly, and persistently. They may feel an internal pressure to keep talking.

4. Flight of Ideas or Racing Thoughts: Thoughts may rush at a quick pace, making it difficult for folks to concentrate on one subject. Their speech may move from topic to issue in a disorganized style.

5. Distractibility: Individuals may find it hard to focus since their attention is easily diverted by irrelevant or insignificant stimuli.

6.Increase in Goal-geared Activity: There may be an increase in activities geared toward accomplishing goals, whether socially, at work, or sexually. This can include starting multiple initiatives but failing to complete them.

7.Excessive Involvement in Pleasurable Activities: Manic episodes frequently entail engaging in activities that have a high potential for negative repercussions, such as excessive spending, unsafe driving, or promiscuous behavior.

Symptoms and Signs of Hypomania

Hypomania is a milder form of mania that is related to bipolar II disorder. While hypomanic episodes share many of the symptoms of mania, they are less severe and do not cause considerable impairment in social or occupational functioning.

Symptoms of Hypomania

Hypomanic episodes last for at least four consecutive days and include the following symptoms:

1. Elevated or Irritable Mood: Similar to mania, hypomania entails a significant shift in mood, which can be elevated, expansive, or irritable.

2. Enhanced Energy and Activity: Individuals often report a jump in energy and activity levels, leading to enhanced productivity and social engagement.

3.Decreased Need for Sleep: Like mania, there is a lessened need for sleep, with individuals feeling rejuvenated after less sleep than usual.

4. Increased Talkativeness: There is generally an increase in verbal communication, with people speaking more fast and more than normal.

5. Raising Thoughts: Individuals may have a quick rush of ideas and thoughts, which can be exhilarating but also distracting.

6. Distractibility: Attention may be readily diverted away from tasks or discussions by irrelevant stimuli.

7.Increase in Goal-Directed Activity: There is typically an increase in activities, particularly those directed at reaching specific goals, which can be useful in moderation.

8. Engagement in Risky Actions: Hypomania can lead to actions that involve some degree of danger, such as increased expenditure or spontaneous decision-making.

Unlike mania, hypomania does not cause severe functional impairment or need hospitalization, but it is nevertheless significant enough to be obvious to others and to signify a divergence from the individual's regular behavior.

Signs and Symptoms of Depression

Depressive episodes are a typical and often devastating feature of bipolar disease, occurring in both bipolar I and bipolar II disorders. These episodes feature lengthy bouts of low mood and a loss of interest or enjoyment in most activities.

Symptoms of Depression

A severe depressive episode involves experiencing five or more of the following symptoms during the same two-week period, with at least one of the symptoms being either a sad mood or a lack of interest or pleasure:

1. Depressed mood: Individuals feel unhappy, empty, or hopeless much of the day, practically every day. This might appear as irritation in children and teenagers.

2. Loss of interest or enjoyment: There is a substantial drop in interest or enjoyment in

practically all activities, most of the day, nearly every day.

3. Significant Weight Change: This can include weight loss when not dieting, weight gain, or a decrease or rise in appetite.

4. Insomnia or hypersomnia: Individuals may experience difficulties sleeping or may sleep excessively.

5. Psychomotor Agitation or Retardation: There can be apparent restlessness or, conversely, delayed bodily motions and speech.

6. Fatigue or Loss of Energy: Persistent tiredness and a loss of energy are prevalent.

7. Feelings of Worthlessness or Guilt: Individuals may experience unwarranted guilt or feel worthless, frequently disproportionately to their actual circumstances.

8. Diminished Ability to Think or Concentrate:

There may be difficulties in thinking, concentrating, or making decisions.

9. Constant Thoughts of Death or Suicide: Which often include suicidal thinking, planning, or attempts.

These symptoms produce severe distress or impairment in social, occupational, or other crucial areas of functioning. Depressive episodes can be life-threatening due to the danger of suicide and require full therapy and care.

Signs and Symptoms of Mixed Episodes

Mixed episodes, or mixed characteristics, occur when symptoms of both mania/hypomania and depression are present simultaneously. These episodes are particularly tough to detect and manage since the co-occurrence of opposing symptoms can lead to severe confusion and anguish.

Symptoms of Mixed Episodes

During a mixed episode, individuals may experience signs of mania or hypomania while also exhibiting symptoms of depression. Some of the main signs include:

1. Manic or Hypomanic Symptoms: These can include enhanced mood, greater energy, decreased need for sleep, increased talkativeness, racing thoughts, distractibility, and increased goal-directed activities.

2. Depressive Symptoms: Simultaneously, individuals may suffer emotions of sorrow, hopelessness, loss of interest or pleasure, exhaustion, feelings of worthlessness or guilt, difficulties concentrating, and suicidal thoughts.

3.Rapid Mood Shifts: Mood may swing fast within the same day, with individuals experiencing extreme highs and lows.

4.irritation and agitation: Mixed episodes frequently accompany a high degree of irritation and physical agitation, making it difficult for individuals to remain calm or focused.

5. Increased Risk of Suicidal Behavior: The presence of both manic and depressive symptoms can considerably raise the risk of suicidal thoughts and behaviors, making mixed episodes particularly risky.

6. Cognitive Impairments: The combination of racing thoughts and depressive cognition can lead to substantial difficulties in concentrating and making judgments.

NOTE:

Understanding the different forms of bipolar disease, including mania, hypomania, depression, and mixed episodes, is critical for a correct diagnosis and efficient treatment. Each type of episode brings unique problems and requires specialized interventions to manage symptoms and improve the quality of life for people affected by bipolar disorder.

Mania

Mania is characterized by an elevated or irritated mood, increased energy, decreased need for sleep, fast speech, racing thoughts, distractibility, heightened goal-directed activities, and dangerous behaviors. It can seriously impede an individual's capacity to function and typically requires rapid care to prevent harm.

Hypomania

Hypomania appears with similar but milder symptoms than mania, lasting for at least four days and not producing severe impairment. It includes enhanced mood, increased energy, talkativeness, racing thoughts, distractibility, and increased activity levels. While less extreme, hypomania nevertheless shows a break from normal behavior and requires monitoring.

Depression

Depressive episodes feature prolonged periods of low mood, loss of interest in activities, weight changes, sleep difficulties, exhaustion, feelings of worthlessness, cognitive deficits, and suicidal thinking. These episodes can be highly debilitating and demand intensive therapy.

Mixed Episodes

Mixed episodes combine signs of mania or hypomania with depression, resulting in rapid mood swings, impatience, agitation, cognitive deficits, and an increased risk of suicidal conduct. These episodes are complex and require careful management to handle the co-occurring symptoms adequately.

By recognizing and separating these episodes, mental health practitioners can make more accurate diagnoses and design effective treatment strategies, ultimately improving outcomes for people living with bipolar disorder.

Chapter 3

Bipolar Disorder Diagnosis

Diagnosing bipolar illness is a comprehensive procedure that includes extensive study and consideration of many aspects. An accurate diagnosis is crucial for appropriate treatment and management of the illness. This detailed review discusses the procedures involved in diagnosing bipolar disorder, including preliminary tests, DSM-5 standards, differential diagnosis, and the importance of physical examinations and medical history.

Preliminary Evaluation: Clinical Interviews and Questionnaires

The initial step in diagnosing bipolar disorder entails a complete preliminary evaluation, which often includes clinical interviews and standardized questionnaires. These instruments assist clinicians in acquiring detailed information about the patient's symptoms, history, and overall mental health status.

Clinical Interviews

Clinical interviews are a cornerstone of the diagnostic process. During these interviews, mental health practitioners participate in structured or semi-structured interactions with patients to assess their mood, behavior, and cognitive performance. Key aspects discussed in clinical interviews include:

1. Symptom History: Clinicians inquire about the presence and duration of symptoms such as mood swings, energy levels, sleep patterns, and changes in behavior. Understanding the timeline and pattern of symptoms is key to recognizing bipolar disorder.

2. Mood Episodes: Detailed information is acquired on any episodes of mania, hypomania,

or despair. Clinicians analyze the severity, frequency, and impact of these episodes on the patient's everyday functioning.

3. Family History: Since bipolar disorder can have a genetic component, clinicians ask about any family history of mood disorders or other psychiatric conditions.

4. Psychosocial Factors: Clinicians analyze the patient's psychosocial environment, including stressors, relationships, and support systems, which can influence mood and behavior.

5.Comorbid diseases: Assessment of other probable mental health diseases, such as anxiety disorders, substance use disorders, or personality disorders, is necessary for appropriate diagnosis and treatment planning.

Questionnaires and Screening Tools

Standardized questionnaires and screening tools supplement clinical interviews by offering a standardized technique for assessing symptoms. Commonly used tools include:

1. Mood Disorder Questionnaire (MDQ) : This self-report questionnaire screens for bipolar disorder by rating the presence and severity of manic and hypomanic symptoms.

2. Beck Depression Inventory (BDI): This tool measures the severity of depression symptoms, helping to identify and differentiate depressive episodes.

3. Young Mania Rating Scale (YMRS): This clinician-administered scale rates the intensity of manic symptoms, aiding in the diagnosis of mania.

4. Hypomania Checklist (HCL-32): This self-report questionnaire screens for hypomanic symptoms and can be beneficial in detecting bipolar II disorder.

These methods, when used alongside clinical

interviews, provide a rigorous framework for screening patients and identifying suspected cases of bipolar illness.

DSM-5 Guidelines for Diagnostic Criteria

The Diagnostic and Statistical Manual of Mental Disorders, Fifth Edition (DSM-5), published by the American Psychiatric Association, defines specific criteria for diagnosing bipolar disorder. The DSM-5 categorizes bipolar disorder into various subgroups, each with specific diagnostic criteria.

Bipolar I Disorder

To diagnose bipolar I disorder, the following criteria must be met:

1. Manic Episode: At least one manic episode is required. A manic episode is defined as a time of unusually and consistently elevated, expansive, or irritable mood, lasting at least one week (or any duration if hospitalization is necessary),

accompanied by at least three (or four if the mood is simply irritable) of the following symptoms:
- Inflated self-esteem or grandiosity; - Decreased desire for sleep; - More chatty than usual or pressure to keep talking; - Flight of ideas or subjective sensation that thoughts are racing; - Distractibility
Improvement in goal-oriented activity or psychomotor agitation; excess participation in activities with a lot potential for painful repercussions

2. Impairment: The manic episode must produce severe impairment in social or occupational functioning, necessitate hospitalization to prevent damage, or contain psychotic symptoms.

Bipolar II Disorder

Bipolar II disorder requires the presence of at least one hypomanic episode and one severe depressive episode.

1. Hypomanic Episode: A time of unusually and consistently elevated, expansive, or irritable mood, lasting at least four consecutive days, accompanied by at least three (or four if the mood is just irritable) of the symptoms listed for mania. However, hypomanic episodes do not cause major impairment in functioning or require hospitalization.

2. Major Depressive Episode: At least one major depressive episode, characterized by five or more of the following symptoms, is present for at least two weeks:
Depressed mood most of the day, practically every day; markedly diminished interest or pleasure in all, or almost all, activities
Significant weight loss or gain, or decrease or increase in appetite
Insomnia or hypersomnia
Psychomotor agitation or retardation; fatigue or loss of energy; feelings of worthlessness or excessive guilt; diminished capacity to focus or concentrate; or indecisiveness; recurrent thoughts of death or suicide

Cyclothymic Disorder

Cyclothymic disorder is diagnosed when the following conditions are met:

1. Chronic Mood Fluctuations: For at least two years (one year in children and adolescents), there have been numerous periods of hypomanic symptoms and depressed symptoms that do not match the criteria for a hypomanic or severe depressive episode.

2.Symptom Persistence: During the two-year period, the mood episodes have been present for at least half the time, and the individual has not been symptom-free for more than two months at a time.

Differential Diagnosis: Setting Apart from Other Mental Health Conditions

Accurately diagnosing bipolar illness includes separating it from other mental health conditions that may appear with similar symptoms. This technique, known as differential diagnosis, is vital to avoid misdiagnosis and provide effective therapy.

Major Depressive Disorder (MDD)

MDD might be tough to discern from the depressed episodes of bipolar illness. Key distinctions include:

1.Presence of Mania or Hypomania: Bipolar disorder involves episodes of mania or hypomania, but MDD does not.

2. Mood Episode Patterns: Bipolar disorder is characterized by recurring mood episodes, comprising highs (mania/hypomania) and lows (depression), whereas MDD comprises mainly depressive episodes.

Anxiety Disorders

Anxiety disorders, such as generalized anxiety

disorder (GAD) and panic disorder, can co-occur with bipolar illness, a confounding diagnosis. Distinguishing features include:

1. Mood Symptoms: Bipolar disorder entails considerable mood fluctuations, while anxiety disorders usually involve excessive worry and fear.

2. Episode Duration and Severity: Manic and depressive episodes in bipolar disorder are more distinct and episodic compared to the chronic nature of anxiety symptoms.

Attention-Deficit/Hyperactivity Disorder (ADHD)

ADHD has symptoms similar to bipolar disorder, such as impulsivity, distractibility, and hyperactivity. Differentiation includes:

1. Symptom Onset and Course: ADHD symptoms are often present from childhood and are chronic, whereas bipolar disorder symptoms

tend to arise later and are episodic.

2. Mood Symptoms: Bipolar disorder involves mood episodes, which are not characteristic of ADHD.

Borderline Personality Disorder (BPD)

BPD and bipolar disorder both entail emotional instability and impulsivity. Key differences include:

1.Mood Episode Duration: Bipolar mood episodes continue for days to weeks, but BPD mood swings can occur within hours.

2. Core Features: BPD is defined by persistent patterns of unstable relationships, self-image, and affect, alongside impulsive conduct.

The Significance of Physical Examination and Medical History

A detailed physical examination and medical

history are key components of the diagnostic process for bipolar illness. These measures help rule out other potential causes of mood problems and ensure a complete picture of the patient's health.

Physical Examination

A comprehensive physical examination might uncover medical disorders that may mimic or exacerbate mood symptoms. Key aspects include:

1. Neurological Examination: Assessing for neurological problems that could alter mood and behavior, such as seizures or brain damage.

2. Endocrine Evaluation: identifying hormonal imbalances, such as thyroid diseases, that can influence mood.

3. drug use assessment: screening for drug usage, which might cause or worsen mood disorders.

Medical History

A complete medical history provides insight into elements that may contribute to mood disorders and informs the diagnosis process. Important components include:

1.Family History: exploring the occurrence of mood disorders or other psychiatric problems in family members, which can indicate a genetic susceptibility.

2. Personal Medical History: reviewing past medical illnesses, surgeries, and treatments that may affect mental health.

3.Medication History: evaluating current and historical medications, including any adverse effects and interactions that could affect mood.

4. Psychiatric History: Documenting previous mental health diagnoses, treatments, and hospitalizations to understand the patient's psychiatric background.

Diagnosing bipolar illness is a difficult process that involves numerous steps to ensure accuracy and appropriate treatment. Preliminary examinations through clinical interviews and standardized questionnaires provide a full review of symptoms and background. Adhering to DSM-5 standards enables an organized and evidence-based approach to diagnosis.

A differential diagnosis is necessary to separate bipolar illness from other mental health conditions with similar presentations, such as major depressive disorder, anxiety disorders, ADHD, and borderline personality disorder. A comprehensive physical examination and extensive medical history further boost diagnostic accuracy by ruling out other probable reasons and evaluating the patient's general health.

Accurate diagnosis of bipolar disorder is critical

for designing successful treatment programs that suit the unique needs of each individual, eventually improving outcomes and quality of life for those affected by this complicated condition.

Chapter 4

Effect on Daily Life

Attention-deficit/hyperactivity disorder, also known as ADHD, is a neurodevelopmental condition that has a substantial impact on day-to-day life conditions. There are a variety of settings in which its symptoms, which include impulsivity, hyperactivity, and inattention, can be observed. These settings include personal interactions, the workplace, educational institutions, and routines for self-care. Having an understanding of how attention-deficit/hyperactivity disorder (ADHD) affects various areas might provide insights into better management tactics and supporting interventions.

The Implications for Individual Relationships

ADHD has the potential to significantly impact personal connections, ranging from the dynamics of families to romantic partnerships and friendships. Individuals with ADHD sometimes have trouble listening, remembering details, and maintaining consistent conduct, which can lead to misunderstandings and frustration.

1. Relationships within the family: Attention-Deficit/Hyperactivity Disorder (ADHD) can put a strain on the relationships between parents and children as well as between siblings. As a result of the need for continual supervision and the difficulty of managing their child's behavior, parents of children with attention-deficit/hyperactivity disorder (ADHD) may feel increased levels of stress. As a result of the increased attention that their brother or sister requires, siblings may experience feelings of being neglected or burdened. It is possible to alleviate some of these problems through the use of effective communication and disciplined

routines; nonetheless, the emotional toll can be very severe.

2. Relationships with a romantic partner: Symptoms of attention-deficit/hyperactivity disorder (ADHD) such as forgetfulness, impulsivity, and distractibility can cause problems in romantic relationships. Partners without ADHD might see these actions as a lack of interest or commitment, producing resentment. Open communication, understanding, and seeking couples therapy can help partners negotiate these problems. Additionally, methods like creating reminders for crucial events or having defined periods for focused communication can improve relationship quality.

3.Friendships: Friendships can also be disrupted since individuals with ADHD may have trouble maintaining consistent contact or remembering social plans. Friends could misunderstand these behaviors as disinterest, leading to potential isolation for the individual with ADHD. To overcome this, friends can establish clear communication routes and be understanding of the occasional lapses in concentration.

Difficulties in Work and School Environments

ADHD creates distinct obstacles in both work and school situations, where productivity and attention to schedules are vital.

1. Workplace Challenges: In professional settings, people with ADHD might struggle with tasks requiring sustained attention, organization, and time management. This can lead to missed deadlines, incomplete projects, and perceived unreliability. Hyperactivity might make it

difficult to stay seated or pay attention during meetings. Employers can support employees with ADHD by establishing flexible work schedules, providing organizational tools, and allowing for movement breaks. Additionally, giving assignments that correspond with the employee's talents and interests might boost productivity.

2. Educational Challenges: In school, children with ADHD often confront issues that can hamper academic performance. They may have problems following instructions, finishing assignments, and remaining focused throughout lessons. This might result in lower academic achievement and unfavorable comments from professors, which can impair their self-esteem. Schools can support kids with ADHD through individualized education plans (IEPs), accommodations like extra time on tests, and adopting teaching approaches that engage many senses to keep attention.

3. Switching Between Tasks: Both at work and school, switching between tasks can be particularly tough for those with ADHD. They could become hyperfocused on one activity at the expense of others or struggle to switch gears, leading to inefficiency. Implementing planned timetables with clear, timed periods for different tasks might help handle these transitions more efficiently.

Organizing Daily Schedules and Self-Care

Managing daily schedules and self-care is critical for those with ADHD, as these areas directly impact their general well-being and capacity to operate well in other facets of life.

1. Creating Structured Routines: A consistent daily routine can provide the required structure to help manage ADHD symptoms. This includes defining specific timings for waking up, eating, working, and sleeping. Using visual tools like calendars, planners, and apps can help track work and appointments. Breaking down huge activities into smaller, achievable chunks can also make them less overwhelming.

2. Implementing Self-Care Practices: Self-care is vital for treating ADHD. Regular physical exercise, a balanced diet, and proper sleep can dramatically improve symptom management. Exercise can reduce hyperactivity and enhance mood, while a healthy diet supports overall brain function. Ensuring a regular sleep schedule can be tough, but it is vital for decreasing symptoms like inattention and irritation. Techniques such as mindfulness and meditation can also help enhance attention and reduce stress.

3. Time Management Strategies: Time management is typically a big difficulty for those with ADHD. Tools such as timers, alarms, and scheduling apps can help keep track of time and ensure chores are accomplished. The Pomodoro Technique, which involves working in focused intervals followed by brief pauses, can be very beneficial. Prioritizing tasks based on urgency and importance can also help manage time more efficiently.

4. Environmental Modifications: Modifying one's environment to avoid distractions might boost productivity and focus. This can include constructing a separate workspace away from extraneous stimulation, utilizing noise-canceling headphones, or working in short bursts with frequent pauses. Organizing physical areas, such as keeping a tidy workstation and using labeled storage, can also lower the cognitive burden and enhance efficiency.

5. Seeking Professional Help: Professional support from therapists, coaches, and medical specialists can provide specific techniques to manage ADHD. Cognitive-behavioral therapy (CBT) can help address negative thought patterns and create coping techniques. ADHD coaches can assist with organization and time management, while medication recommended by a doctor can help regulate symptoms.

ADHD severely impacts various elements of everyday life, from personal relationships to work and educational contexts and the capacity to manage daily schedules and self-care. By acknowledging these problems and employing focused techniques, individuals with ADHD can enhance their quality of life and better navigate the complexities connected with their disease. Support from family, friends, employers, and experts plays a critical role in this process, providing an atmosphere where individuals with ADHD can thrive.

Chapter 5

Care and Handling(ADHD)

Attention-deficit/hyperactivity disorder (ADHD) is a difficult neurodevelopmental ailment that necessitates a comprehensive strategy for treatment and control. Effective management includes pharmaceutical drugs, various psychotherapy modalities beyond cognitive-behavioral therapy (CBT) and dialectical behavior therapy (DBT), lifestyle adjustments, and the crucial role of support systems. Understanding these individual features can help those with ADHD experience fulfilling lives.

Pharmacological Therapies:

Drugs and Their ApplicationsPharmacological treatment is a cornerstone in the management of ADHD. Medications can greatly lessen fundamental symptoms such as inattention, hyperactivity, and impulsivity, thereby increasing daily functioning.

1. Stimulant Medications: The most often prescribed medications for ADHD are stimulants, which include amphetamine-based drugs (e.g., Adderall, Vyvanse) and methylphenidate-based drugs (e.g., Ritalin, Concerta). These medications enhance the levels of specific neurotransmitters in the brain, such as dopamine and norepinephrine, which can improve attention and focus while lessening hyperactive and impulsive tendencies. They are useful in around 70–80% of patients with ADHD but can have negative effects, including insomnia, appetite loss, and increased heart rate.

2. Non-stimulant medicines: For those who do not respond well to stimulants or experience unpleasant side effects, non-stimulant drugs offer an option. Atomoxetine (Strattera) is a selective norepinephrine reuptake inhibitor that can help manage symptoms without the potential

for addiction associated with stimulants. Other non-stimulant alternatives include guanfacine (Intuniv) and clonidine (Kapvay), which are primarily used to treat high blood pressure but also diminish ADHD symptoms by lowering the brain's receptors for norepinephrine.

3. Antidepressants: Sometimes, antidepressants like bupropion (Wellbutrin) are prescribed for ADHD, particularly when there is a co-occurring mood disease. These medications function by changing neurotransmitters such as dopamine and norepinephrine, enabling symptom alleviation for both ADHD and depression.

4. Considerations for Medication Management: The choice of drug and dosage is highly individualized, necessitating close coordination between the patient and healthcare practitioner. Regular monitoring for effectiveness and unwanted effects is crucial, as is altering the treatment strategy as needed. Combining

medicine with behavioral therapy can increase overall outcomes.

Alternatives to CBT and DBT in Psychotherapy

While CBT and DBT are well-known therapy treatments for ADHD, numerous other psychotherapies can also be effective.

1. Mindfulness-Based Therapy: Mindfulness practices aid individuals with ADHD in achieving awareness and acceptance of their thoughts and feelings. Mindfulness-based cognitive therapy (MBCT) combines normal cognitive therapy with mindfulness activities to help reduce symptoms of ADHD and increase emotional regulation. Techniques such as mindful breathing and meditation can increase focus and lessen impulsivity.

2. Neurofeedback: Neurofeedback, sometimes known as EEG biofeedback, is a technique that trains individuals to regulate their brain wave

patterns. By offering real-time feedback on brain activity, neurofeedback helps individuals learn to increase brain activity associated with focus and decrease activity linked to distraction and impulsivity. This non-invasive therapy has exhibited potential for boosting attention and reducing hyperactivity in patients with ADHD.

3.Interpersonal Therapy (IPT): IPT focuses on developing interpersonal ties and social functioning, which can be troublesome for persons with ADHD. This therapy helps individuals understand how their interactions with others affect their mental health and offers ways to improve communication, resolve disagreements, and establish stronger relationships.

4. Art and Music Therapy: Creative therapies like art and music therapy provide alternative ways to express and process emotions, which can be particularly beneficial for children and adolescents with ADHD. These therapies can

boost self-esteem, reduce stress, and improve focus and self-discipline through controlled creative activities.

Adjustments to Lifestyle and Practices for Self-Management

Lifestyle adjustments and self-management tactics are crucial components of ADHD care. These approaches enable patients to control their symptoms and boost their quality of life.

1. Regular Routines: Establishing and following a regular daily pattern can help individuals with ADHD manage their time more productively. This includes setting exact hours for waking up, eating, working, exercising, and sleeping. Using planners, calendars, and apps to keep track of work and appointments can provide more support.

2. Diet and Nutrition: A balanced diet can have a good impact on ADHD symptoms. Diets high in protein, complex carbohydrates, and omega-3

fatty acids can help balance energy levels and promote cognitive function. Limiting sugar and processed foods can minimize hyperactivity and impulsivity.

3. Exercise: Regular physical exercise is effective for managing ADHD symptoms. Exercise can enhance dopamine levels, enhancing mood, focus, and attention. Activities such as cardiovascular activities, yoga, and martial arts can be very effective.

4. Sleep Hygiene: Good sleep hygiene is crucial, as sleep issues are frequent in individuals with ADHD. Establishing a consistent sleep routine, establishing a quiet bedtime ambiance, and avoiding stimulants like caffeine before bed will help boost sleep quality

5. Mindfulness and Relaxation Techniques: Incorporating mindfulness and relaxation techniques into everyday activities can help individuals with ADHD manage stress and boost focus. Practices such as meditation, deep breathing exercises, and progressive muscular

relaxation help reduce anxiety and increase emotional regulation.

The Value of Support Systems

Support systems play a crucial role in the treatment and management of ADHD. These methods provide emotional, practical, and social aid, which can considerably boost results for those with ADHD.

1. Family Support: Families are often the largest support system for individuals with ADHD. Educating family members about ADHD and engaging them in treatment strategies helps enhance understanding and cooperation. Family therapy can also be effective in addressing any relational issues and boosting communication.

2. Peer Support: Peer support groups provide a platform for individuals with ADHD to exchange experiences, concerns, and coping strategies. These organizations offer a sense of kinship and understanding, minimizing feelings

of loneliness. Both in-person and online support groups are available and can be wonderful aids.

3. School help: For students with ADHD, help inside the school system is crucial. This includes concessions such as extended time on tests, breaks during class, and access to tutoring or academic coaching. Teachers and school counselors can work collaboratively with parents and students to build individualized education plans (IEPs) that meet unique needs.

4. Workplace Support: Employers can support individuals with ADHD by providing accommodations such as flexible work hours, the ability to work from home, and access to organizing tools. Supervisors can also offer regular feedback and guidance, helping staff manage their workload and stay on track.

5. Professional Support: Working with experts such as therapists, ADHD coaches, and medical providers is crucial for comprehensive care. These professionals can provide specialized techniques, therapeutic treatments, and

pharmacological management to help individuals with ADHD handle their everyday problems.

Effective care and handling of ADHD require a multimodal strategy that combines pharmaceutical medication, alternative psychotherapies, lifestyle adjustments, and good support systems. By incorporating these variables, individuals with ADHD can better control their symptoms, improve their quality of life, and fulfill their personal and professional goals. Understanding the numerous techniques and supports available enables a more tailored and successful management strategy, enhancing resilience and success for those living with ADHD.

Chapter 6

Living with Bipolar Disorder

Bipolar illness, a mental health condition marked by significant mood swings between manic/hypomanic and depressed episodes, dramatically impacts individuals and their families. Understanding lived experiences, effective coping strategies, and available services can provide valuable insights into managing this complicated condition.

Individual Narratives and Case Studies

Personal accounts and case studies of individuals living with bipolar disorder offer unique views on the struggles and triumphs linked with the condition.

1. Case Study 1: Sarah's Journey: Sarah, a 32-year-old graphic designer, was diagnosed with bipolar I disorder at the age of 25. She

recalls experiencing her first manic episode during college, characterized by limitless energy, quick speaking, and reckless actions. This was followed by a major depressive episode, leading to hospitalization. With the support of her family and a dedicated mental health team, Sarah started a treatment plan that included mood stabilizers and psychotherapy. Over time, she learned to notice early warning signals of mood fluctuations and developed coping mechanisms such as maintaining a rigorous sleep schedule, engaging in regular exercise, and practicing mindfulness. Today, Sarah successfully manages her condition, keeps a steady job, and promotes mental health awareness in her community.

2. Case Study 2: Mark's Experience: Mark, a 45-year-old teacher, was diagnosed with bipolar II disease in his early 30s. His hypomanic bouts, distinguished by enhanced productivity and creativity, often went unnoticed, but his depressive episodes substantially hindered his capacity to work. Mark's turning point came when he sought therapy following a particularly

debilitating depressive episode. Through a mix of medication, cognitive-behavioral therapy (CBT), and support groups, Mark achieved better control over his symptoms. He emphasizes the significance of routine and has found consolation in hobbies like painting and gardening. Mark's story shows the necessity of early intervention and the role of community support in controlling bipolar disease.

3. Case Study 3: Maria's Story: Maria, a 28-year-old entrepreneur, suffered her first significant depressive episode in her late teens, followed by a manic episode during her early twenties. After repeated misdiagnoses, she was finally diagnosed with bipolar I disease. Maria battled with medication adherence due to side effects but eventually discovered a combination that worked for her. She credits her success to a holistic approach, combining medication with lifestyle modifications like a nutritious diet, regular physical activity, and keeping a strong support network. Maria's entrepreneurial energy drove her to design a mental health app to assist

people in managing their moods and medication adherence, turning her problems into a source of inspiration for others.

Coping and Thriving Techniques

Living with bipolar disorder involves a complete strategy for surviving and thriving, combining medical treatment, lifestyle adaptations, and psychological interventions.

1. Medication Management: Adhering to a recommended medication regimen is vital for regulating mood fluctuations. Common drugs include mood stabilizers (e.g., lithium, valproate), antipsychotics (e.g., olanzapine, quetiapine), and antidepressants (e.g., SSRIs, SNRIs). Regular appointments with a psychiatrist are required to check effectiveness and alter dosages as needed. Individuals should discuss honestly with their healthcare professionals any adverse effects or concerns.

2.Psychotherapy: Various forms of

psychotherapy can help people manage bipolar disorder. Cognitive-behavioral therapy (CBT) supports recognizing and correcting negative thought patterns, whereas interpersonal and social rhythm treatment (IPSRT) focuses on maintaining regular daily routines and enhancing interpersonal interactions. Psychoeducation is also beneficial, helping individuals understand their illness and create effective coping techniques.

3. Lifestyle Modifications: Establishing a consistent routine is crucial for those with bipolar disorder. Consistent sleep habits, regular meals, and organized activities help control mood. Exercise is particularly useful since it decreases stress, enhances mood, and increases overall well-being. Mindfulness techniques, such as meditation and yoga, help promote emotional regulation and reduce anxiety.

4. Stress Management: Learning to handle stress is crucial for preventing mood crises. Techniques like deep breathing exercises, progressive

muscular relaxation, and indulging in hobbies might help reduce stress levels. Avoiding alcohol and recreational drugs is also vital, as these substances can provoke mood episodes.

5. Support Networks: Building and sustaining strong support networks is vital. Family, friends, and support groups provide emotional support and practical assistance. Open conversation about one's health and requirements can enhance these connections and develop understanding.

6. Self-Monitoring: Keeping a mood diary can help individuals track their mood changes, identify triggers, and spot early warning signs of episodes. Apps built for mood tracking might offer handy ways to monitor symptoms and exchange data with healthcare providers.

Resources for Individuals and Families

A multitude of resources are available to support individuals with bipolar disorder and their families, ranging from instructional materials to support services and advocacy groups.

1. Educational Resources: Websites like the National Institute of Mental Health (NIMH) and the Mayo Clinic provide comprehensive information about bipolar disorder, including symptoms, treatment choices, and coping strategies. Books such as "An Unquiet Mind" by Kay Redfield Jamison and "The Bipolar Disorder Survival Guide" by David J. Miklowitz give personal insights and practical assistance.

2. Support Groups: Organizations like the Depression and Bipolar Support Alliance (DBSA) and the National Alliance on Mental Illness (NAMI) offer peer-led support groups, both in-person and online. These groups provide a secure area for individuals to share experiences, receive support, and learn from others facing similar issues.

3. Therapy and counseling care: access to competent mental health care is vital. Many therapists specialize in treating bipolar disorder

and can provide individual, group, or family therapy. Telehealth programs have also improved access to mental health care, allowing individuals to get support from the comfort of their homes.

4. Crisis Resources: Immediate support is available through crisis hotlines like the National Suicide Prevention Lifeline and Crisis Text Line. These programs provide 24/7 access to experienced counselors who can offer support and direction during challenging times.

5. Financial Assistance: Managing bipolar disorder can be costly, but many programs and services can help. Medicaid and Medicare offer coverage for mental health services, and the Substance Abuse and Mental Health Services Administration (SAMHSA) provides information on low-cost treatment choices. Nonprofit groups and foundations may also offer financial support for medication and therapy.

6. Employment Support: The Americans with

Disabilities Act (ADA) provides protections for individuals with bipolar illness in the workplace. Employers are expected to make reasonable accommodations, such as flexible work hours and modified duties. Vocational rehabilitation services can also assist people in finding and retaining employment.

7. Advocacy and knowledge: Advocacy organizations aim to raise knowledge of bipolar disease and battle stigma. Participating in awareness campaigns, sharing personal stories, and supporting mental health legislation can contribute to broader public understanding and acceptance.

Living with bipolar disorder poses substantial obstacles, but with the correct combination of medical treatment, psychotherapy, lifestyle adaptations, and support systems, individuals can manage their disease effectively and have satisfying lives. Personal anecdotes and case studies reflect the different experiences of people with bipolar disorder, stressing the significance of tailored care. Coping and thriving approaches, such as medication management, therapy, lifestyle adjustments, and stress management, are critical components of comprehensive care. Access to resources, including educational materials, support groups, therapeutic services, and financial assistance, further empowers individuals and their families. By embracing these tools and resources, people living with bipolar disorder can navigate their journey with strength and hope.

Chapter 7

Current Research and Upcoming Paths

Bipolar disorder, characterized by episodes of mania and sadness, offers considerable challenges to individuals and healthcare systems worldwide. Traditionally addressed with pharmaceutical and psychological approaches, modern research is exposing new insights and prospective therapeutic options. This essay goes into the newest discoveries in the study of bipolar disorder, including genetic studies, neuroimaging advancements, novel therapy methods, digital health interventions, the gut-brain axis, epigenetics, precision medicine, and initiatives to expand access to care.

Genetic Research and Biomarkers

A considerable focus in contemporary research is on the genetic origins of bipolar disorder.

Genome-wide association studies (GWAS) have revealed multiple genetic variations connected with the illness. These studies demonstrate that bipolar disorder is polygenic, indicating that numerous genes contribute to its development. Notably, mutations in genes such as CACNA1C, which encodes a calcium channel component, have been related to the condition. This gene's significance in calcium signaling, critical for neuronal activity, offers prospective avenues for targeted therapeutics.

ANK3, another gene associated with bipolar disease, impacts neuronal stability. Understanding how these genetic differences contribute to bipolar disorder's pathophysiology could lead to more effective treatments. Additionally, researchers are examining biomarkers, including inflammatory cytokines, neurotrophic factors, and oxidative stress indicators, to predict mood episodes and treatment responses. Integrating genetic data with biomarker research shows potential for personalized medicine, providing therapies tailored to individual genetic profiles and biomarker markers.

Neuroimaging and Brain Circuitry

Advancements in neuroimaging techniques such as functional MRI (fMRI) and positron emission tomography (PET) are altering our understanding of brain abnormalities in bipolar disorder. These techniques enable researchers to observe and measure brain activity and connection, revealing insights into the neuronal networks involved in mood regulation.

Studies have discovered anomalies in the prefrontal cortex, amygdala, and hippocampus—regions crucial for emotional regulation, memory, and executive function. A reduced connection between the prefrontal cortex and amygdala, for instance, may cause difficulty controlling emotional reactions in patients with bipolar disorder. Volumetric investigations have also shown losses in gray matter in these locations, possibly linked to the neurodevelopmental components of the illness.

Emerging neuroimaging research is studying neuroinflammation's function in bipolar illness. PET scans have indicated increased microglial activation, a hallmark of neuroinflammation, in the brains of individuals during manic and depressive episodes. This shows that neuroinflammation may contribute to bipolar disorder's pathogenesis, making it a possible target for innovative anti-inflammatory therapy.

Novel Therapeutic Approaches

Traditional medications for bipolar disorder, such as lithium, antipsychotics, and mood stabilizers, can be beneficial but typically have considerable side effects and unpredictable efficacy. Consequently, there is a pressing need for novel therapeutic techniques that are more successful and have fewer unwanted effects.

One intriguing area of investigation is glutamatergic agents. Glutamate, the major excitatory neurotransmitter in the brain, has been implicated in bipolar disorder due to dysregulation of its signaling. Ketamine, a glutamate receptor antagonist, has shown fast antidepressant effects in people with treatment-resistant depression, including those with bipolar disorder. Researchers are now researching the therapeutic potential of various glutamatergic drugs, such as NMDA receptor modulators and AMPA receptor potentiators, for both manic and depressive phases.

Neuromodulation treatments, such as transcranial magnetic stimulation (TMS) and transcranial direct current stimulation (tDCS), also show potential for modifying brain activity and alleviating mood symptoms. These non-invasive approaches target specific brain regions involved in mood regulation, presenting viable alternatives for those who do not react to pharmaceuticals.

Psychotherapy and Digital Health Interventions

While medicine remains a cornerstone of bipolar disorder treatment, psychotherapy is vital in treating the disease. Recent research focuses on enhancing existing psychotherapy treatments and establishing new interventions targeted to the special needs of people with bipolar disorder.

Cognitive-behavioral treatment (CBT) has been tailored to address the special issues of bipolar disorder, emphasizing mood monitoring, cognitive restructuring, and lifestyle regularity. Psychoeducation programs have been helpful in boosting treatment adherence and reducing relapse rates by teaching patients and their families about the disorder and management techniques.

The emergence of digital health technologies offers new options for offering psychotherapy and assisting individuals with bipolar disorder. Mobile apps and online platforms can provide psychoeducation, mood monitoring, and therapeutic interventions, making mental health help more accessible. These digital solutions can provide real-time mood tracking, helping users detect mood trends and triggers, permitting early intervention. Additionally, digital health treatments provide a platform for remote therapy, addressing barriers such as geographical distance and stigma associated with obtaining mental health care.

The Gut-Brain Axis

A new topic of research in bipolar illness is the exploration of the gut-brain axis, which refers to the bidirectional contact between the gastrointestinal tract and the central nervous system, mediated by neuronal, hormonal, and immunological pathways.

Recent research suggests that the gut microbiota—the billions of microorganisms in the intestines—may play a role in mental health, including bipolar disorder. Dysbiosis, an imbalance in the gut microbiota, has been related to several psychiatric illnesses, and researchers are now examining its impact on bipolar disorder.

Animal studies have revealed that modifying the gut microbiota can influence behavior and brain function, presumably through processes such as immune regulation and the generation of neuroactive chemicals. Preliminary research in humans has discovered changes in gut microbiota composition between people with bipolar disorder and healthy controls.

Probiotics and prebiotics, which affect gut flora, are being examined as potential supplementary therapies for bipolar illness. Clinical trials are underway to examine these therapies' effects on mood symptoms and general mental health. The gut-brain axis represents a breakthrough frontier in bipolar disorder research, bringing new insights into the condition's basic underpinnings and prospective therapeutic options.

Epigenetics and Environmental Factors

While hereditary variables play a substantial role

in bipolar disorder, environmental factors and their interaction with genetic predispositions are equally critical in its development. Epigenetics, the study of changes in gene expression that do not entail mutations in the DNA sequence, provides a framework for understanding how environmental variables influence the risk and course of bipolar disorder.

Recent research has found many epigenetic mechanisms, such as DNA methylation and histone modification, that may contribute to the pathophysiology of bipolar disorder. Studies have indicated altered DNA methylation patterns in genes associated with the hypothalamic-pituitary-adrenal (HPA) axis and neuroplasticity in people with bipolar disorder. These findings imply that stress and other environmental factors may change gene expression, thereby influencing brain function and mood regulation.

Understanding the epigenetic landscape of bipolar disorder could lead to the development of epigenetic treatments aiming to reverse or change abnormal gene expression patterns. Such medicines could offer a fresh way to treat bipolar disease, perhaps improving outcomes for patients who do not respond to standard medications.

Precision Medicine and Personalized Treatment

The integration of genetic, neuroimaging, biomarker, and clinical data paves the path for precision medicine methods in bipolar disorder. Precision medicine strives to personalize treatments for individual patients based on their unique biology and clinical profiles, rather than taking a one-size-fits-all approach.

Pharmacogenomics, the study of how genetic variations influence an individual's reaction to drugs, is an important area of attention. By identifying genetic markers related to treatment response and adverse effects, researchers hope to build guidelines for individualized medicine selection and administration. For instance, differences in the CYP450 enzymes, which metabolize many psychiatric drugs, can impact treatment efficacy and tolerance. Pharmacogenomic testing could help clinicians identify the most effective and safe drugs for each patient.

Precision medicine concepts are now being applied to non-pharmacological treatments. Neuroimaging and electrophysiological data, for example, could identify individuals most likely to benefit from neuromodulation procedures like TMS or electroconvulsive therapy (ECT). Similarly, individualized psychotherapy interventions could be constructed based on an individual's cognitive and emotional characteristics.

Addressing Disparities and Enhancing Access to Care

Despite progress in understanding and treating bipolar disease, discrepancies in access to care and treatment results exist. Socioeconomic level, race, ethnicity, and geographic location influence an individual's capacity to obtain and benefit from mental health care. Addressing these discrepancies is critical for improving outcomes for all individuals with bipolar disorder.

Current research is examining measures to promote access to care and reduce inequities. Telepsychiatry, which employs telecommunication technology to provide psychiatric services remotely, shows promise in reaching disadvantaged communities. Telepsychiatry can overcome hurdles such as geographical distance and limited access to mental health experts, particularly in rural and low-income areas.

Additionally, community-based therapies and integrated care models are being created to provide comprehensive and culturally appropriate care. These models stress collaboration between mental health specialists, primary care providers, and community organizations to serve the complex needs of patients with bipolar disorder. By integrating mental health care into primary care settings and harnessing community resources, these methods aim to enhance access to care and facilitate long-term recovery.

The research on bipolar illness is experiencing a change, spurred by breakthroughs in genetics, neuroimaging, novel therapy methods, digital health interventions, the gut-brain axis, epigenetics, precision medicine, and initiatives to expand access to care. These breakthroughs give new insights into the disorder's pathophysiology and hold the potential to revolutionize its management. As research improves, the merging of these varied techniques promises to lead to more effective, tailored, and accessible therapies, ultimately improving outcomes for people with bipolar disorder.

Chapter 8

Upcoming Trends in the Diagnosis and Treatment of Bipolar Disorder

Bipolar disorder, marked by extreme mood swings ranging from mania to depression, continues to pose significant challenges in diagnosis and treatment. Recent advancements in medical research and technology are paving the way for more accurate diagnostic methods and innovative treatments. This essay explores the upcoming trends in the diagnosis and treatment of bipolar disorder, highlighting advancements in genetic research, neuroimaging, digital health, pharmacotherapy, psychotherapeutic approaches, the gut-brain axis, precision medicine, and efforts to reduce disparities in healthcare.

1. Genetic Research and Personalized Medicine

A growing body of research is focused on understanding the genetic basis of bipolar disorder. Genome-wide association studies (GWAS) have identified numerous genetic variants associated with the disorder. These discoveries are crucial for developing personalized medicine approaches that tailor treatments to an individual's genetic makeup.

Key genes, such as CACNA1C and ANK3, have been linked to bipolar disorder. CACNA1C is involved in calcium signaling, which is essential for neuronal communication. Variations in this gene may affect mood regulation, making it a potential target for new therapies. Similarly, ANK3 is associated with neuronal stability and signal transmission, suggesting that drugs targeting this pathway could be beneficial.

Biomarkers are also gaining traction as tools for diagnosis and treatment planning. For example, inflammatory markers, neurotrophic factors, and oxidative stress indicators are being studied to predict mood episodes and treatment responses. Combining genetic information with biomarker profiles can lead to more precise and effective treatments, moving beyond the traditional trial-and-error approach.

2. Neuroimaging Advances

Neuroimaging techniques, such as functional MRI (fMRI) and positron emission tomography (PET), are revolutionizing our understanding of brain abnormalities in bipolar disorder. These tools allow researchers to visualize brain activity and connectivity, providing insights into the neural circuits involved in mood regulation.

Studies have identified structural and functional abnormalities in regions like the prefrontal cortex, amygdala, and hippocampus. For instance, reduced connectivity between the prefrontal cortex and amygdala may underlie difficulties in emotional regulation seen in bipolar disorder. Volumetric studies have also noted reductions in gray matter in these areas, highlighting the neurodevelopmental aspects of the disorder.

Emerging neuroimaging research is exploring the role of neuroinflammation in bipolar disorder. PET scans have revealed increased microglial activation, a marker of neuroinflammation, in the brains of individuals during manic and depressive episodes. This finding suggests that targeting neuroinflammation could be a novel therapeutic approach.

3. Digital Health and Remote Monitoring

Digital health technologies are transforming the landscape of bipolar disorder diagnosis and treatment. Mobile apps and wearable devices can provide continuous monitoring of mood, activity levels, and sleep patterns. These tools enable real-time tracking of symptoms, helping individuals and healthcare providers identify mood changes and potential triggers.

Telemedicine is another promising trend, particularly for reaching underserved populations. Telepsychiatry can provide remote consultations and therapy sessions, making mental health care more accessible. This approach is especially beneficial for individuals in rural areas or those who face barriers to in-person care.

Artificial intelligence (AI) and machine learning are also being integrated into digital health platforms. AI can analyze data from various sources, such as electronic health records, social media activity, and wearable devices, to predict mood episodes and recommend interventions. These technologies can support personalized treatment plans and early intervention, potentially reducing the severity and frequency of mood episodes.

4. Innovations in Pharmacotherapy

Pharmacological treatment of bipolar disorder has traditionally relied on mood stabilizers, antipsychotics, and antidepressants. However, these treatments often have significant side effects and variable efficacy. Recent research is exploring novel pharmacological agents that target specific pathways implicated in bipolar disorder.

One promising area is the development of glutamatergic agents. Glutamate is the primary excitatory neurotransmitter in the brain, and dysregulation of glutamatergic signaling has been implicated in bipolar disorder. Ketamine, a glutamate receptor antagonist, has shown rapid antidepressant effects in individuals with treatment-resistant depression, including those with bipolar disorder. Researchers are now investigating other glutamatergic agents, such as NMDA receptor modulators and AMPA receptor potentiators, for both the manic and depressive phases of the disorder.

Another area of interest is neurosteroids, which modulate the activity of neurotransmitter receptors. Allopregnanolone, a neurosteroid, has shown promise in treating depression and anxiety. Clinical trials are underway to evaluate its efficacy in bipolar disorder, particularly for rapid symptom relief.

5. Advanced Psychotherapeutic Approaches

Psychotherapy remains a cornerstone of bipolar disorder management, complementing pharmacotherapy. Cognitive-behavioral therapy (CBT) has been adapted to address the specific challenges of bipolar disorder, focusing on mood monitoring, cognitive restructuring, and lifestyle regularity.

Recent innovations include the development of specialized psychotherapeutic approaches tailored to different phases of the disorder. For example, interpersonal and social rhythm therapy (IPSRT) emphasizes the stabilization of daily rhythms and interpersonal relationships, which can help prevent mood episodes. Similarly, family-focused therapy (FFT) involves educating family members about the disorder and developing strategies to support the individual with bipolar disorder.

Digital psychotherapy is also emerging as a valuable tool. Online platforms and mobile apps can deliver evidence-based psychotherapeutic interventions, making therapy more accessible and convenient. These platforms often include interactive modules, mood tracking, and personalized feedback, enhancing engagement and adherence.

6. The Gut-Brain Axis

The gut-brain axis is an emerging area of research in bipolar disorder, highlighting the bidirectional communication between the gastrointestinal tract and the central nervous system. Gut microbiota—the trillions of microorganisms residing in the intestines—are thought to influence brain function and behavior.

Studies have found differences in gut microbiota composition between individuals with bipolar disorder and healthy controls. Dysbiosis, an imbalance in the gut microbiota, has been linked to various psychiatric conditions, including bipolar disorder. Researchers are investigating how these microbial communities influence mood regulation, potentially through immune modulation and the production of neuroactive compounds.

Probiotics and prebiotics, which modulate the gut microbiota, are being explored as potential adjunctive treatments for bipolar disorder. Clinical trials are underway to evaluate the effects of these interventions on mood symptoms and overall mental health. The gut-brain axis represents a novel and promising frontier in bipolar disorder research, offering new insights into the biological mechanisms underlying the disorder and potential therapeutic targets.

7. Epigenetics and Environmental Factors

Epigenetics, the study of changes in gene expression that do not involve alterations in the DNA sequence, is providing new insights into how environmental factors influence bipolar disorder. Epigenetic mechanisms, such as DNA methylation and histone modification, can be affected by stress, diet, and other environmental factors, potentially altering brain function and mood regulation.

Recent research has identified altered DNA methylation patterns in genes related to the hypothalamic-pituitary-adrenal (HPA) axis and neuroplasticity in individuals with bipolar disorder. These findings suggest that stress and other environmental factors may play a significant role in the disorder's development and course.

Understanding the epigenetic landscape of bipolar disorder could lead to the development of epigenetic therapies, which aim to reverse or modify pathological gene expression patterns. Such therapies could offer a novel approach to treating bipolar disorder, potentially improving outcomes for individuals who do not respond to conventional treatments.

8. Precision Medicine

The integration of genetic, neuroimaging, biomarker, and clinical data is paving the way for precision medicine approaches in bipolar disorder. Precision medicine aims to tailor treatments to individual patients based on their unique biological and clinical profiles, rather than adopting a one-size-fits-all approach.

Pharmacogenomics, the study of how genetic variations influence an individual's response to medications, is a key area of focus. By identifying genetic markers associated with treatment response and side effects, researchers hope to develop guidelines for personalized medication selection and dosing. For example, variations in the CYP450 enzymes, which metabolize many psychiatric medications, can affect drug efficacy and tolerability. Pharmacogenomic testing could help clinicians choose the most effective and safe medications for each patient.

Precision medicine approaches are also being applied to non-pharmacological treatments. Neuroimaging and electrophysiological data, for example, could identify individuals most likely to benefit from neuromodulation techniques like TMS or electroconvulsive therapy (ECT). Similarly, personalized psychotherapeutic interventions could be developed based on an individual's cognitive and emotional profiles.

9. Addressing Disparities and Enhancing Access to Care

Despite advances in understanding and treating bipolar disorder, disparities in access to care and treatment outcomes persist. Socioeconomic status, race, ethnicity, and geographic location influence an individual's ability to access and benefit from mental health services. Addressing these disparities is crucial for improving outcomes for all individuals with bipolar disorder.

Current research is exploring strategies to enhance access to care and reduce disparities. Telepsychiatry, which uses telecommunication technology to provide psychiatric services remotely, shows promise in reaching underserved populations. Telepsychiatry can overcome barriers such as geographical distance and the limited availability of mental health professionals, particularly in rural and low-income areas.

Community-based interventions and integrated care models are being developed to provide comprehensive and culturally sensitive care. These models emphasize collaboration between mental health professionals, primary care providers, and community organizations to address the multifaceted needs of individuals with bipolar disorder. By integrating mental health care into primary care settings and leveraging community resources, these approaches aim to improve access to care and support long-term recovery.

10. Social and Cultural Considerations

Cultural and social factors play a crucial role in the diagnosis and treatment of bipolar disorder. Cultural perceptions of mental health can influence how individuals seek help, their adherence to treatment, and their interactions with healthcare providers. Recognizing and addressing these factors is essential for providing effective and culturally competent care.

Research is increasingly focusing on understanding the cultural context of bipolar disorder.

Conclusion

Bipolar disease, distinguished by its violent mood swings between mania and despair, is a complex and frequently devastating condition. However, new developments in study and treatment offer a ray of hope for individuals suffering from this illness. This conclusion includes crucial information from the newest research and breakthroughs and provides inspiration and hope for anyone living with bipolar disease and their loved ones.

Highlights of Important Information

1. Genetic Research and Personalized Medicine

Understanding the genetic roots of bipolar disease has been a prominent emphasis in recent years. Genome-wide association studies (GWAS) have found many genetic variations associated with the illness, such as CACNA1C and ANK3, which play essential roles in neuronal communication and stability. This genomic understanding paves the path for customized medicine, where therapies can be matched to an individual's genetic profile. Biomarker research, including inflammatory markers and oxidative stress indicators, further strengthens our ability to anticipate mood episodes and treatment responses, leading towards more accurate and effective management of the condition.

2. Advances in Neuroimaging

Neuroimaging tools like functional MRI (fMRI) and positron emission tomography (PET) have considerably advanced our understanding of the brain abnormalities associated with bipolar disorder. Research has shown structural and functional abnormalities in key brain regions involved in mood regulation, such as the prefrontal cortex, amygdala, and hippocampus. Additionally, investigations on neuroinflammation utilizing PET scans have shown increased microglial activation during manic and depressive episodes. These data show that addressing neuroinflammation could be a promising new treatment approach.

3. Digital Health and Remote Monitoring

Digital health technology is altering how we manage bipolar disorder. Mobile apps and wearable devices offer continuous monitoring of mood, activity, and sleep patterns, providing real-time data that assists in the early detection of mood swings. Telepsychiatry is making mental health care more accessible, especially for individuals in remote or underdeveloped locations. Furthermore, artificial intelligence (AI) and machine learning are being integrated into digital health platforms, enabling predictive analytics and individualized treatment suggestions.

4. Innovations in Pharmacotherapy

Traditional medication for bipolar disorder comprises mood stabilizers, antipsychotics, and antidepressants. Recent advances are addressing glutamatergic medicines, which target the key excitatory neurotransmitter glutamate, implicated in bipolar illness. Ketamine, a glutamate receptor antagonist, has shown fast antidepressant effects, and research is ongoing to create new glutamatergic drugs. Neurosteroids like allopregnanolone are also being explored for their ability to quickly improve mood disorders.

5. Advanced Psychotherapeutic Approaches

Psychotherapy remains an important component of bipolar disorder treatment. Cognitive-behavioral therapy (CBT) has been adapted to address specific issues of the illness, focusing on mood monitoring and lifestyle regularity. Newer techniques like interpersonal and social rhythm therapy (IPSRT) and family-focused therapy (FFT) focus on stabilizing daily rhythms and enhancing interpersonal connections. Digital psychotherapy platforms are making these interventions more accessible and engaging, boosting adherence and outcomes.

6. The Gut-Brain Axis

The gut-brain axis is an emerging area of research that highlights the relationship between gut microbiota and brain function. Dysbiosis, or an imbalance in the gut microbiota, has been linked to psychiatric illnesses like bipolar disorder. Researchers are researching probiotics and prebiotics as potential adjunctive therapies that could regulate gut flora and enhance mood symptoms. This unique technique gives new insights into the molecular basis of bipolar disease and prospective treatment targets.

7. Epigenetics and Environmental Factors

Epigenetics explores how environmental influences regulate gene expression without modifying the DNA sequence. Recent research has demonstrated that stress, food, and other variables can impact epigenetic systems like DNA methylation, influencing brain function and mood regulation. Understanding these epigenetic modifications could lead to new therapeutics that modify abnormal gene expression patterns, offering hope for individuals who do not react to standard treatments.

8. Precision Medicine

Precision medicine strives to adapt treatments to individual patients based on their unique genetic, neuroimaging, biomarker, and clinical data. Pharmacogenomics, which examines how genetic variations affect medicine's response, is a critical component. By discovering genetic markers connected to therapy efficacy and side effects, doctors can personalize pharmaceutical regimens. Precision medicine also extends to non-pharmacological treatments, employing neuroimaging and electrophysiological data to identify candidates for neuromodulation procedures like transcranial magnetic stimulation (TMS) and electroconvulsive therapy (ECT).

9. Addressing Disparities and Enhancing Access to Care

Despite progress, discrepancies in access to care and treatment outcomes exist. Socioeconomic status, race, ethnicity, and geographic location can all affect access to mental health services. Strategies like telepsychiatry and community-based therapies attempt to eliminate these discrepancies by delivering comprehensive, culturally sensitive care. Integrating mental health care into primary care settings and harnessing community resources can enhance access and assist long-term rehabilitation.

10. Social and Cultural Considerations

Cultural and societal factors strongly influence the diagnosis and treatment of bipolar disorder. Understanding cultural perspectives on mental health can assist healthcare workers in providing more effective and culturally competent care. Research focusing on the cultural context of bipolar disorder is vital for designing interventions that resonate with varied communities and eliminate the stigma associated with mental health problems.

Inspiration and Hope for People Affected by Bipolar Disorder

While bipolar disorder can be tough, the continual improvements in research and therapy give tremendous hope and inspiration for people affected by the condition. Here are some reasons for optimism:

1. Personalization of Treatment

The drive towards customized medicine means that individuals with bipolar disorder can receive therapies tailored to their own genetic and clinical characteristics. This technique offers more efficacy and fewer adverse effects, improving overall treatment outcomes. Personalized medicine acknowledges the individuality of each patient, boosting the potential for prolonged recovery and well-being.

2. Early Detection and Intervention

Advances in digital health and remote monitoring provide instruments for early detection and intervention. Continuous tracking of mood and activity through mobile apps and wearable devices can help spot early indicators of mood swings, allowing for prompt interventions. Early intervention is vital in minimizing the escalation of symptoms and lowering their impact on everyday life.

3. Innovative Therapies

The development of innovative pharmacological drugs and neuromodulation techniques offers new possibilities for treatment, especially for people who do not react to standard medicines. Glutamatergic drugs and neurosteroids represent intriguing prospects in pharmacology, while TMS and other neuromodulation techniques provide non-invasive choices for symptom alleviation. These developments expand the treatment toolset available to doctors and patients.

4. Accessibility of Care

Telepsychiatry and digital psychotherapy platforms are making mental health care more accessible, particularly for people in remote or underserved locations. These technologies break down obstacles such as geographical distance and stigma, making it easier for people to seek and receive the care they need. Greater accessibility guarantees that more people can benefit from excellent therapies and assistance.

5. Comprehensive and Culturally Sensitive Care

Efforts to reduce gaps in mental health care have led to the creation of more comprehensive and culturally sensitive care models. By integrating mental health treatments into primary care and using community resources, these models provide holistic assistance that addresses the complex needs of individuals with bipolar disorder. Culturally responsive treatment acknowledges the different experiences of patients, creating trust and boosting engagement.

6. Empowerment Through Knowledge

Increased awareness of the biological and environmental elements contributing to bipolar disease empowers individuals with knowledge about their condition. Education and psychoeducation programs help patients and their families understand the disease, notice early warning signs, and create appropriate coping methods. Knowledge is a great tool for controlling bipolar disorder and establishing long-term stability.

7. Research and Advocacy

Ongoing research and advocacy activities continue to push the frontiers of what is known about bipolar disorder and how it can be treated. Organizations and researchers dedicated to mental health are tirelessly trying to improve diagnostic methods, discover novel therapies, and promote awareness. These efforts not only increase scientific understanding but also remove stigma and encourage acceptance and support for people living with bipolar disorder.

8. Community and Support Networks

Building and sustaining strong support networks is vital for those with bipolar disorder. Family, friends, healthcare providers, and support groups play a crucial role in offering emotional support, practical assistance, and encouragement. Connecting with individuals who understand the struggles of bipolar disease helps develop a sense of belonging and lessen feelings of isolation.

9. Hope for the Future

The future of bipolar illness therapy is bright, with continual developments promising more effective, tailored, and accessible care. As research continues to reveal the complexity of the disorder and develop creative solutions, individuals with bipolar disorder can look forward to better management options and an improved quality of life. The dedication of scientists, physicians, and advocates inspires optimism that one day bipolar disorder will be fully understood and efficiently managed, allowing sufferers to enjoy satisfying and productive lives.

The landscape of bipolar disorder diagnosis and treatment is rapidly altering, giving fresh hope and possibilities. The convergence of genetic research, neuroimaging, digital health, novel medicines, and customized medicine is revolutionizing how bipolar disease is understood and controlled. Efforts to expand access to care and address cultural and socioeconomic concerns are ensuring that more people receive the support they need. For those suffering from bipolar disorder, these breakthroughs offer a message of inspiration and optimism: brighter days are ahead, and with

continuous progress, the burden of this severe
condition can be considerably eased.

* 9 7 9 8 3 2 7 1 1 2 4 5 2 *